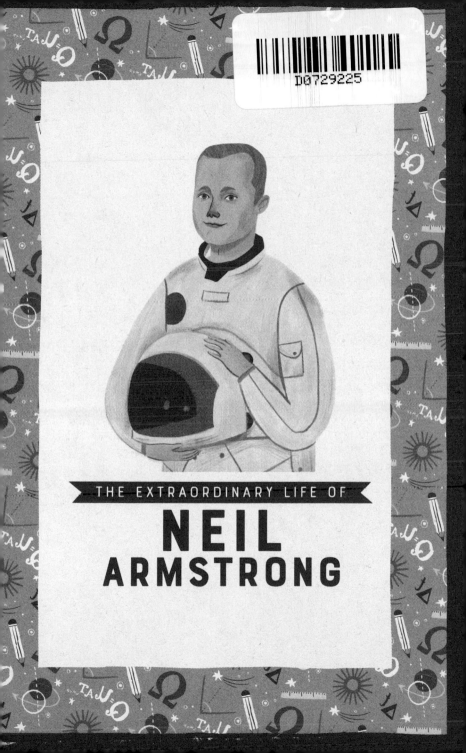

THE EXTRAORDINARY LIFE OF

NEIL
ARMSTRONG

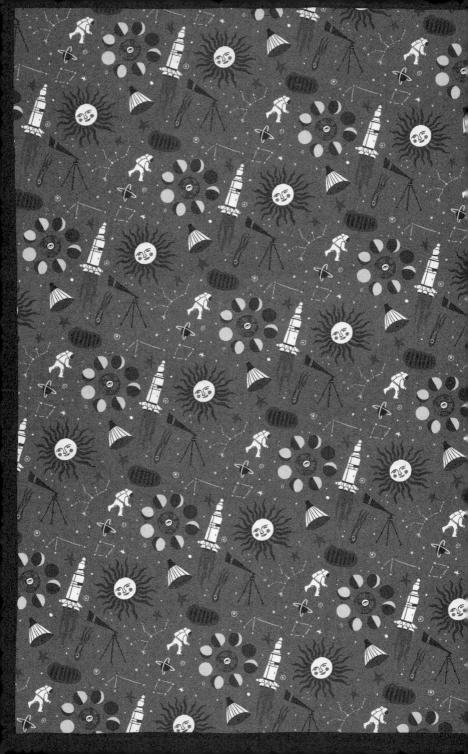

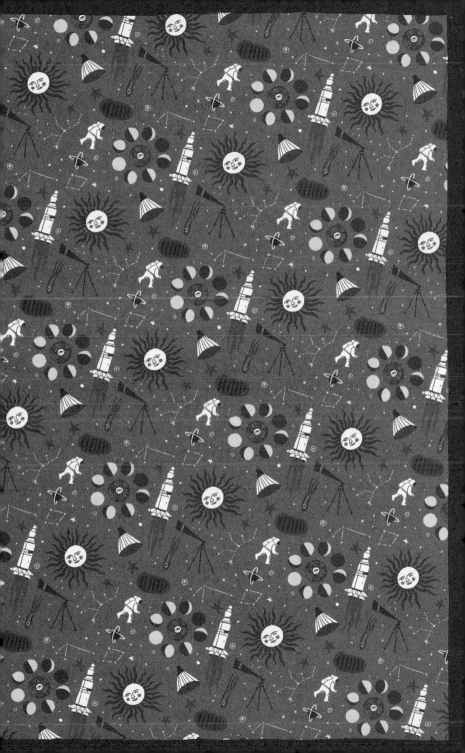

First American Edition 2020
Kane Miller, A Division of EDC Publishing

Original edition first published by Penguin Books Ltd, London
Text copyright © Martin Howard 2019
Illustrations copyright © Freda Chiu 2019
The author and the illustrator have asserted their moral rights.

All rights reserved. No part of this publication may be reproduced, stored in
a retrieval system, or transmitted, in any form or by any means, electronic,
mechanical, photocopying, recording or otherwise, without the prior
permission of the publisher and copyright owner.

For information contact:
Kane Miller, A Division of EDC Publishing
P.O. Box 470663
Tulsa, OK 74147-0663
www.kanemiller.com
www.edcpub.com
www.usbornebooksandmore.com

Library of Congress Control Number: 2019942941

Printed and bound in the United States of America
2 3 4 5 6 7 8 9 10
ISBN: 978-1-68464-073-7

THE EXTRAORDINARY LIFE OF
NEIL
ARMSTRONG

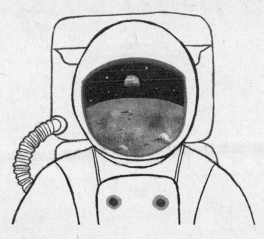

Written by Martin Howard
Illustrated by Freda Chiu

Kane Miller
A DIVISION OF EDC PUBLISHING

WHO WAS
Neil
Armstrong?

On July 20, 1969, at 10:56 p.m. eastern daylight time (EDT), a man stepped off a *ladder*. Around the world 530 million people held their breath and watched a black-and-white image on boxy, old-fashioned televisions. The man was *Neil Armstrong*, commander of the Apollo 11 space mission, and at the bottom of the ladder was the *surface* of the *moon*.

When he first set foot on the moon Neil Armstrong was thirty-eight years old. He was a quiet ENGINEER and pilot who once described himself as a "nerd."

Neil's step was one of the most important and extraordinary in human history. With one footstep he showed that humanity's voyages of discovery could continue out into space.

ENGINEER: someone who designs and makes machinery.

MOONWALKERS:
A VERY SMALL CLUB

You could probably fit all the people who have ever walked on the moon into your bedroom. So far there have been only twelve, including Neil Armstrong.

The moon landing was not Neil's achievement alone. Back in the landing craft – called the lunar module, or Eagle – his copilot, **Buzz Aldrin**, was waiting to follow him down.

Miles above, **Michael Collins** was ORBITING the moon in the command module called Columbia, waiting to take them home again.

ORBIT:
to go around and around something. All the planets in the solar system orbit the sun.

The moon is a *satellite* (something that travels around Earth), or a "celestial body," or an "astronomical body."

Back on Earth thousands of people, from presidents to engineers, had made incredible *efforts* to prepare for the journey. It had cost the American people *billions* of dollars to get all three men to the moon. But this was Neil Armstrong's moment, a moment that made him one of the most *famous* people on Earth, and a moment that would be *remembered* for all time.

"I think we're going to the moon because it's in the nature of the human being to face challenges."

Small steps

The boy who would one day walk on the moon was born near a small town called **Wapakoneta**, in Ohio, on August 5, 1930. The **oldest** of three children, Neil had a happy childhood.

His father, Stephen, moved around a lot for his work as an AUDITOR. By the time Neil was fourteen the family had moved sixteen times, ending up back in Wapakoneta.

AUDITOR: a person who does an audit, checking a company's accounts.

Everywhere the family went, Neil made friends easily. People liked him. He read a lot, and was a **quiet** kid who didn't much enjoy being the center of **attention**, but he was clever, honest, often funny and easy to get along with.

The world was a different place back then. No one had television – only **radio**. Anyone who predicted humans would reach the moon within the next forty years would have been laughed at. The idea of putting a human in **space** was for mind-boggling popular **adventure magazines** with titles like *Astounding Stories* and *Cosmic Science Fiction*.

DID YOU KNOW?

While Neil was growing up in sleepy Ohio, horse-drawn wagons were still as common as cars!

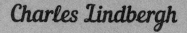

Charles Lindbergh

But most people had thought *flying* was impossible too. Yet by the time Neil was born **airplanes** were a worldwide craze. In 1927 **Charles Lindbergh** became the first person to fly across the Atlantic Ocean.

SPIRIT OF ST. LOUIS

Amelia Earhart

He was followed a year later by **Amelia Earhart**, the first woman to achieve this amazing feat. Neil grew up in a world where flight was the greatest **adventure** that could be dreamed of, and he soon had his own eyes on the sky.

"OLD BESSIE"

Neil went to his first **air show** when he was two, and loved playing with toy airplanes. Although he liked music and became a keen Boy Scout, flying machines were his first love.

By the time he was eight Neil spent every spare moment building model planes from wood and tissue paper, powering their PROPELLERS with rubber bands. Over the years he built hundreds.

PROPELLER:

a blade that spins around at high speed.
Before the jet engines you see on planes nowadays,
all planes were powered by propellers.

DID YOU KNOW?

The United States of America entered the Second World War in 1941 when Neil was eleven years old. He got involved with the US war effort by making model airplanes. They were so good that the military used them to teach new recruits the differences between enemy and friendly aircraft.

By the age of fifteen Neil was working part-time in a local store, and he used the money for *flying lessons*. He took the exam for his pilot's license on his sixteenth birthday.

Neil was overjoyed when, in 1947, he was accepted to study AIRCRAFT ENGINEERING at Purdue University in Indiana.

AIRCRAFT ENGINEERING:
the study of how to make airplanes.

Neil's education was paid for by the United States Navy (the part of the military that commands ships and submarines). In return he would have to join the navy for three years after his first two years in college.

By this time the world was **changing**. Fast. Scientists and engineers were building jet aircraft and **rockets** that could go faster and higher than ever before. People were finally starting to believe that space flight might become a reality.

The choices Neil made when he was young were leading him toward the moon. Joining the navy was one of the most important. Many of the first astronauts were navy pilots with engineering experience, and a *navy pilot* with an *engineering degree* is exactly what Neil Armstrong would become.

Jet engines

"That was very exciting for me,
to be in the front lines of
THE NEW JET FIGHTERS."

*N*eil's first year in college went well, but in January
1949, Neil was told his navy *training* would start early.

Eighteen-year-old Neil entered the navy in Pensacola, Florida, on February 24, 1949. For almost two years he was given training in planes that were much *faster* and more *difficult* to fly than he was used to. In early 1951 he was chosen to train in one of the navy's new jet airplanes. It was an opportunity he had been longing for. Jets were fast and Neil loved the *thrill* of flying at high speed.

By the end of June Neil's aircraft-carrier ship was sailing to Korea where the US was fighting a war. There Neil would fly seventy-eight missions over *enemy* territory. It was daring work that needed courage and skill.

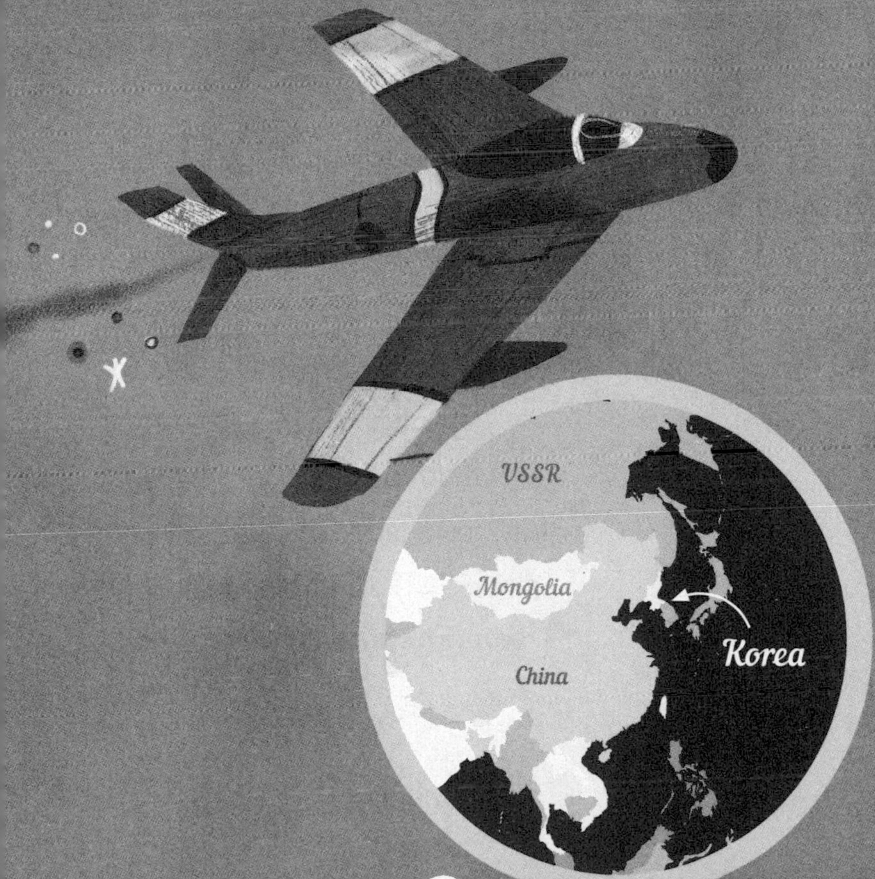

USSR

Mongolia

China

Korea

Once, Neil's plane was involved in an accident that sliced three feet off the jet's wing. Neil managed to pilot the damaged plane back to friendly territory where he *parachuted* to safety.

DID YOU KNOW?

In 1951 Neil flew his plane over a mountain ridge in Korea and saw a field of unarmed enemy soldiers exercising. Neil could have killed many of them with his jet's machine guns. But he took his finger off the trigger and flew on. He couldn't bring himself to shoot defenseless men.

Neil flew his last war mission on March 5, 1952. During his eight months in Korea he had come close to death many times, but – for Neil – the war was over. For his *service* he was awarded a number of *medals*. More importantly, his superior officers thought he was a *brilliant* pilot with a *cool head*. More pieces of Neil's future were falling into place.

"I AM,
and ever will be,
a WHITE SOCKS,
pocket-protector,
NERDY ENGINEER."

POCKET PROTECTOR:

used by people who carry pens in the front pockets of their shirts. The pocket protector is a small pouch that fits inside the pocket to protect the shirt from being stained if ink leaks from the pen.

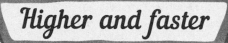

*B*y 1955 Neil had earned his degree in aircraft engineering with **excellent** marks.

There was only one choice of job for a young man who loved flying and engineering. Neil applied to NACA to become a **test pilot**.

NACA:
the National Advisory Committee for Aeronautics.

In 1947 Chuck Yeager had become the first person ever to travel faster than the SPEED OF SOUND. Since then, NACA had been testing new planes that could reach higher and higher speeds.

SPEED OF SOUND: the speed any noise takes to travel across a distance. At 761 miles per hour it's pretty fast!

DID YOU KNOW?

In 1962 Neil flew a plane alongside Chuck Yeager. Neil tried to land the plane on a dry lake bed, only to find that it wasn't as dry as he thought! The wheels got stuck in the mud and the two men had to be rescued. Neil could only sit and scowl while Chuck Yeager laughed at him.

Before starting his new job, Neil went back to Purdue University where he'd met a young woman called *Janet Shearon*. They got married in January 1956.

Not long after, Neil started his *new job* at Edwards Air Force Base.

Soon Neil was helping to launch *skyrocket experimental planes* at Edwards. This was difficult, and *dangerous*. The aircraft couldn't take off on their own and had to be *carried* into the sky by a much bigger plane.

A lot could go *wrong*. Neil soon had the chance to showcase his *quick thinking* while he was flying a large plane (a B-29 Superfortress) with a skyrocket underneath.

One of his engines failed. With its faulty engine screaming, Neil **pushed** the plane into a **dive** and the skyrocket underneath managed to launch. A second later, one of Neil's engines *exploded* and two others failed. Even though he had only one engine, and his controls were almost useless, Neil managed to land *safely*.

Neil stayed at Edwards Air Force Base for **seven years**, testing new aircraft.

When did Neil first wear a spacesuit?

Neil first wore a spacesuit in August 1957 when he made his first flight in a **rocket-powered aircraft**, the Bell X-1B, which went 11.4 miles into the sky.

Back on the ground, important people were taking notice of the brilliant pilot who could coolly take an experimental aircraft to the edge of **space**.

In 1958 NACA became NASA – the National Aeronautics and Space Administration. It had orders from the president to take the US into *space*.

Neil was chosen to try a new experiment. He was strapped into a *pod* at the end of a fifty-foot arm. The pod was then *whirled* around like a carnival ride.

The aim of the experiment was to find out if pilots could still use controls under the same kind of G-FORCES that would be produced when riding a rocket into space.

G-FORCE:

gravitational force, the feeling of being heavier when you go from stationary to moving fast, very quickly. If you've ever been on an airplane taking off or on a roller coaster going down a steep slope, you'll know it's like being pushed back in your seat. Taking off in a rocket is like that, but the force pushing you back in your seat is *much* bigger!

The space race

*A*t the beginning of the 1960s the US and Russia were in competition to see who would be the first to conquer space. The US was losing. In October 1957, Russia had launched the first *satellite* – called Sputnik 1. A few years later, in April 1961, the Russian astronaut *Yuri Gagarin* became the first human ever to go into *space*, *orbiting* Earth in space capsule Vostok 3KA.

Yuri Gagarin

In September 1962, President John F. Kennedy announced that the US would land a *man on the moon* before the end of the decade.

"BUT WHY, SOME SAY, THE MOON?
Why choose this as our goal?
AND THEY MAY WELL ASK,
why climb the highest mountain?
Why, THIRTY-FIVE YEARS AGO,
fly the Atlantic? . . .

WE CHOOSE TO GO TO THE MOON in this *decade* and do the other things, NOT BECAUSE THEY ARE EASY, but because **they are hard . . .** BECAUSE THAT *challenge* IS ONE THAT WE ARE WILLING TO ACCEPT . . . "

— John F. Kennedy

Putting a man on the moon would be a stunning show to amaze the whole world (especially the Russians!).

Neil had considered applying to become an **astronaut**, but – at first – he thought his test-pilot work at Edwards was more important. When he found out that NASA was looking for new astronauts in 1962, though, he changed his mind and sent in an **application**.

Neil's astronaut application arrived at NASA's Manned Spacecraft Center in Houston, Texas, **a week late**. It should have been thrown out, but one man there already knew Neil. He thought Neil would make a great astronaut, and slipped the letter into the pile of applications without anyone knowing!

Over the next few months Neil was given many **tests**.

Some of the tests were just plain weird. Once he had ice-cold water squirted into his ear. Another test meant sitting in a dark, silent room for hours.

In September 1962, Neil got a phone call. NASA had accepted him as an astronaut, along with *eight* other men. The plan to put men on the moon was named the Apollo program, or *Project Apollo*, and President Kennedy was right: it was a very tough mission. At that time the technology and equipment needed to make such an incredible *journey* just didn't exist.

"There wasn't **anybody** THAT HAD DONE THIS and could tell us HOW TO DO IT, because *nobody* HAD THE EXPERIENCE."

Everything from rockets and new fuels to computers and spacesuits had to be *designed* from scratch. So NASA launched *Project Gemini* to create and test everything that would be needed to get to the moon and back. Neil, the geeky engineer, was interested in lots of the work and even helped solve some of the problems facing the designers.

Before Neil could take his first flight into space he was given *extreme training*. Astronauts had to learn different kinds of *math* too, as well as be trained in all the equipment they would be using.

DID YOU KNOW?

Part of an astronaut's training takes place in an airplane that swoops down from a great height. For about thirty seconds at a time everyone inside is weightless. So many people are sick on their first flight that the plane is nicknamed the "Vomit Comet"!

In March 1966, Gemini 8, with Neil as commander, blasted off. At his side was pilot David Scott. It was their first journey into space. Their mission was to dock with an unmanned spaceship, meaning two spaceships had to meet up and connect. It was the first time this had ever been tried, and was hugely important for Project Apollo. To drop onto the moon's surface, a landing craft would have to be used. Later, it would have to launch from the surface and dock with the main spaceship waiting above. If docking failed, the men on board the landing craft would have no way to get back to Earth.

Neil Armstrong and David Scott did it perfectly. Everyone at Houston Mission Control whooped with joy. Then David Scott's voice came over the radio:

"WE HAVE SERIOUS *problems here.*"

Their ship had begun to tumble out of control. Neil quickly undocked from the unmanned ship. He still couldn't control the Gemini ship. One of its THRUSTERS was stuck open, making it spin wildly. To make matters worse, they lost radio contact with Earth.

THRUSTER:
a small rocket on a spaceship, which is used to make changes in speed and direction.

Anyone else **might have panicked**, but Neil activated the controls for taking the craft back to Earth, brought the Gemini ship back under his control and shut down the faulty thruster.

By the time Houston Mission Control center got the two astronauts on the radio again, Neil had **saved the ship**, and his and David Scott's lives. Their mission was over, though. Neil had orders to prepare for an immediate return to Earth.

"SAVE YOUR CRAFT, save the crew, GET BACK HOME and be disappointed THAT YOU HAD TO leave some of your goals BEHIND."

Countdown

*I*t was more than three years before Neil went back into **space**. Project Gemini, which tested the new technology needed to send people to the moon, ended in 1966. Project Apollo – which would achieve the actual moon landing – was on. Over the next three years its space flights would get closer and closer to that final goal.

In December 1968, Apollo 8 **orbited** the moon without making a landing. In March 1969, a mission to test the lunar module – the little craft that would make the moon landing – was also a success, although it didn't touch down on the moon.

DID YOU KNOW?

The Apollo 8 mission took place over Christmas 1968. As the world watched this miracle on TV, commander Jim Lovell said,

"Please be informed, there is a Santa Claus."

Neil Armstrong's next flight into space was to be the *Apollo 11* mission. At the time no one was **certain** that Apollo 11 would be the mission that landed on the moon. If anything had gone wrong with the Apollo 8, 9 or 10 missions, the landing would have been pushed back to Apollo 12 or 13. But it soon became clear that Neil would be in command of the actual *moon landing*. He would be taking *Buzz Aldrin* and *Michael Collins* as his crew members.

When the world learned who would be manning Apollo 11, the first question the media asked was *"Who will be the first to set foot on the moon?"*

It was decided that Neil Armstrong would be the one to take this historic step. Buzz would follow him down to the lunar surface a few minutes later, and Michael would wait in the command module above to take them back to Earth.

To Neil, it was the mission that mattered, not the fame.

"The important thing was THAT WE GOT FOUR ALUMINUM LEGS *down safely on* THE SURFACE OF THE MOON."

Americans say "aluminum" while the British say "aluminium." The chemist who discovered it, Sir Humphry Davy, named it twice before sticking to "aluminium" – "aluminum" was his second attempt!

The Apollo 10 mission was a full **"dress rehearsal"** for the moon landing, a final check that all systems were ready – without landing on the moon's surface. Neil and his fellow crew members listened on the radio while the crew launched the landing craft, checked that they could fly it above the surface of the moon, and then flew back to dock with the command module. Apollo 10 returned to Earth with all its crew alive and well. The mission was a total success. NASA announced that the Apollo 11 astronauts had been told to attempt a **landing on the moon**.

*O*n the morning of July 16, 1969, Neil Armstrong, Michael Collins and Buzz Aldrin took an *elevator* to the top of the Saturn V rocket that would shoot them into the sky.

At more than 360 feet tall, the Saturn V rocket was more than twice as tall as the Statue of Liberty!

For miles around, the roads, beaches and open spaces were *packed* with people, all staring at the shining white rocket in the distance.

Neil's wife, Janet, and their two sons watched from a special boat on the nearby *Banana River*. Millions more around the world were glued to their TVs. The three astronauts were strapped into their seats in Columbia, the command module, and connected to oxygen supplies.

The crew took oxygen with them to stay alive in space, where there isn't any air to breathe.

Just before he entered Columbia, Neil gave a ticket he'd made to the man in charge of the launchpad. The ticket read, "SPACE TAXI: GOOD BETWEEN ANY TWO PLANETS."

At 9:32 a.m. EDT, Saturn V's engines boomed. In Columbia, Neil, Michael and Buzz were almost deafened by the roar. Slowly at first, but quickly gaining speed, the rocket **blasted** up through Earth's atmosphere.

"*Ignition sequence starts.*

10,
9,
8,
7,
6,
5,
4,
3,
2,
1,
0.

ALL ENGINES RUNNING.

Liftoff! We have a *liftoff!*

THIRTY-TWO MINUTES PAST THE HOUR.

Liftoff on Apollo 11!"

– Jack King, NASA chief of public information

Outside the window of the command module the sky deepened from blue to the black of space. As the rocket left Earth's atmosphere, the ride smoothed out and Columbia entered Earth's orbit.

The crew had two hours and fifteen minutes to check that everything on their ship was working. They also had to get the lunar module out of its container and dock with it, so it was ready to be used. After they finished, the rocket's engines sent Columbia toward the moon faster than a bullet. Its job done, the third stage of the rocket was dumped. The huge metal tube spun away into space.

The moon is *238,855 miles* away from Earth. Even whizzing through space at super-high speed, it takes more than three days to get there.

Floating in the command module, Neil, Michael and Buzz climbed out of their bulky spacesuits and ate special packs of food made for ZERO GRAVITY. Behind them Earth grew slowly smaller.

ZERO GRAVITY:

out in space, away from Earth, there is no gravity holding astronauts down, so they float around in their spaceships. Sometimes called zero-g.

The crew were kept busy with *chores*, making sure that nothing aboard Columbia went wrong. They also had a camera to *film* each other for people back on Earth. Neil talked about what he could see of Earth from space and did *headstands* in zero gravity.

Meanwhile, Buzz did zero gravity push-ups and Michael made a chicken stew. When he wasn't filming or working, Neil listened to *music* and looked out of the window to see the silver-gray moon getting *bigger* by the hour.

Food in space

It's difficult to eat and drink in space because of the lack of gravity. Even water wouldn't stay in a cup – it would float around! The food and drink needed to provide all the right nutrients and be easy to store and eat. It was often dried and then put into vacuum packs.

After their third night's sleep in space, Neil and his crew awoke with an *important* job to do. They began the tricky task of putting Columbia into orbit around the moon. This meant slowing down and *approaching* from exactly the right angle. If they weren't accurate, the ship could skip past the moon and head straight on toward the sun. It was difficult piloting.

When Columbia disappeared around the dark side of the moon, radio contact with Earth was lost.

Everyone knew that contact would be lost for a short time. Radio waves couldn't travel **around** or **through** the moon, and Mission Control were prepared for Neil and his crew being unable to communicate.

For *twenty-three minutes* there was silence from Apollo 11. Mission Control in Houston also fell silent. People around the world stared silently at their TV screens.

(NOT TO SCALE)

FLIGHT PATH

RADIO SILENCE WHEN THE MOON OBSCURED APOLLO 11'S RADIO WAVES

MOON

APOLLO 11

EARTH

It was a terrifying twenty-three minutes. Had everything gone to plan, or was the spaceship *hurtling* toward the fiery sun? Slowly the minutes ticked down.

And then Houston picked up a *signal*. Apollo 11 swung around and back into range. Quickly Neil reported that the ship had successfully entered the moon's orbit. He used a lot of complicated math and talked about angles and speeds and fuel burn. Mission Control asked him to repeat it. Neil simplified his report for them:

"It was like – like perfect."

Touchdown

$\mathcal{E}$very part of the Apollo 11 mission was dangerous, but nothing was as *risky* as the moon landing itself. While Michael Collins stayed aboard Columbia, Neil and Buzz were to pilot the lunar module – Eagle – down to the surface.

NASA had made it clear that no rescue mission would be possible if something went wrong. If they crashed or couldn't make it back to Columbia, the cameras would be turned off. The president had even prepared a speech in case Neil and Buzz had to be left to die on the moon.

On the morning of July 20, Neil and Buzz entered Eagle. Neil flew it a short distance away, then fired thrusters so the small craft spun in front of Columbia's window. Michael looked it over carefully, checking everything he could see. Finally he said, "You're looking good."

"Roger. Eagle's undocked. The Eagle has wings."

DID YOU KNOW?

The lunar module was so small that there was no room for seats. While Eagle dropped 60 miles to the moon's surface, Neil and Buzz had to stand up.

The landing site the Apollo 11 crew had chosen was an area of the moon called the SEA OF TRANQUILITY, which looked smooth and safe for landing.

THE SEA OF TRANQUILITY: this isn't a sea as we know it. It's a lunar mare – a large plain formed long ago by a volcanic eruption.

Eagle looped around the moon and slowly dropped into position for the final descent. Neil checked they were in the right place using a SEXTANT.

SEXTANT: an old-fashioned navigation instrument used by sailors since the eighteenth century.

Neil and Buzz made final checks. The last thing they did was switch on a camera.

Once again, thrusters fired. Eagle began to drop toward the moon. Inside, Neil watched the moon's surface. He soon realized that the module was going to miss its landing-site target.

At the time he didn't think this was a problem. He fired the thrusters again, bringing Eagle upright, with its four feet ready to touch the surface. Then an alarm went off. The computer had *overloaded*.

Neil reported the problem to Houston. When Eagle was about 650 yards from the surface and dropping fast, another computer alarm came on. Neil ignored it. Having come so far he didn't want to abort the mission because of a computer crash.

DID YOU KNOW?

Computer technology in the 1960s wasn't as advanced as it is today. The computers the Apollo 11 crew worked with were far less powerful than today's mobile phones.

Neil could see that Eagle wasn't going to land where he had planned. He realized the landing site was going to be a *lot* more rocky than he had hoped for.

At around 50 yards above the surface he picked a new landing spot. Eagle skimmed over rocks the size of cars. Any of them could easily have destroyed the craft. By now, though, Neil had other problems. Fuel was running low and Eagle's thrusters were swirling up a fog of dust from the moon's surface, making it ***impossible*** to see where he was landing.

"STAND BY FOR THIRTY SECONDS,"

said Mission Control. There was only thirty seconds' worth of fuel left.

Skillfully Neil guided the lunar module down to a landing so *gentle* that he and Buzz hardly felt the bump as their spaceship settled on the surface of the moon.

"Houston,
TRANQUILITY BASE HERE.
The Eagle has landed."

For all humankind

*F*or the first time human beings had traveled to a place beyond Earth. It was an *extraordinary* moment in history.

Across the globe people cheered, cried with relief, goggled at their TV sets in amazement, opened bottles of champagne and prayed.

Hundreds of thousands of miles above them, Neil just shook Buzz Aldrin's hand and said,

"OK, let's get on with it."

But first he and Buzz had to make sure that Eagle was ready to take off again. Then they ate a meal of bacon and peaches. In fact, it was more than six hours before Neil **opened** Eagle's hatch, climbed onto the ladder outside and stepped down onto the **moon**.

Letting go of the ladder and setting his left foot on the ground, Neil said his now-famous words.

"THAT'S one small step for man. ONE GIANT LEAP for mankind."

DID YOU KNOW?

Neil was supposed to say
"THAT'S ONE SMALL STEP FOR **A** MAN."
He forgot to say "A" – but that's understandable!
Neil Armstrong was cool, but even for him
it was a mind-blowing moment.

Neil looked out over the **landscape** through the visor of his helmet: a gray, lifeless desert of craters and rocks and powdery dust the color of ash. He thought it was **beautiful** in its own way. Almost the only color to be seen was Earth, which hung against the blackness of space like a blue jewel swirled with clouds.

"IT SUDDENLY **struck** ME THAT that tiny *pea,* PRETTY AND BLUE, *was the* **Earth.** I PUT UP MY THUMB *and* SHUT ONE EYE, AND MY ***thumb*** *blotted out* THE *planet* **Earth.** I DIDN'T FEEL LIKE A GIANT. *I felt very, very small."*

Neil was holding the shared camera for most of their time on the moon, so the only photo of Neil on the moon is a reflection in Buzz's visor.

A few minutes after Neil had stepped off the ladder, Buzz joined him on the *surface*. Because of the moon's low gravity, normal walking was difficult, so they ended up half walking, half hopping.

DID YOU KNOW?

Gravity on the moon is only **one-sixth** as strong as gravity on Earth. If you jumped on the moon, you'd go **six times higher!**

Both Neil and Buzz had a list of things to do. First, they unveiled a plaque on one of the lunar module's legs (the landing gear would stay on the moon). Over the radio Neil told the people of Earth what it said:

"Here men from the planet Earth first set foot on the moon, July 1969 AD. We came in peace for all mankind."

One of the things they did next was set up an American flag. After that, Mission Control put a phone call through to them from President Nixon.

Neil and Buzz also collected samples of moon rock, and set up experiments. After about **two and a half hours** Mission Control told them it was time to end their moonwalk. Buzz climbed back aboard Eagle and ten minutes later Neil followed. Just before they closed the hatch, they threw out patches commemorating Russian and American astronauts who had died, and a golden olive branch – a symbol of peace. Inside, the two men refilled the lunar module with oxygen so they could take off their **spacesuits**. Both noticed that Eagle now smelled different, from the dust that had come through the hatch with them. For the first time they were *smelling* the moon. According to Neil and Buzz it smells like wet ashes.

The two of them checked Eagle's systems and ate another meal. Then they settled down to sleep. Mission Control woke them seven hours later.

After nearly a day spent on the moon the time came for Eagle to return to Columbia for the trip home. Blasting off from the moon and joining back up with the spaceship above them was another *dangerous* and tricky job. Hundreds of things could go wrong and any one of them would mean Michael would have to leave Neil and Buzz behind.

Takeoff went smoothly. The tiny craft rose from the moon, leaving its landing gear behind.

The docking took three *very* tense hours. In the end though, the crew had only one problem. As the two craft joined, Michael hit a switch too quickly. Eagle began to spin away from Columbia. Fortunately all three men were ace pilots and corrected the mistake.

Covered in **moondust**, Neil and Buzz tumbled through the hatch into Columbia. Equipment and samples were transferred to the spaceship, and Eagle was sent on its final journey: orbiting the moon for a few years before crashing back to the surface. The most dangerous part of the mission was over, and it had been an **amazing success**. All that lay ahead was the long journey back to Earth.

DID YOU KNOW?

Neil Armstrong may have been the first man to set foot on the moon but Buzz Aldrin was the first man to go to the bathroom there, using a special tube in his spacesuit!

"I was
ELATED,
ecstatic and
EXTREMELY SURPRISED
that we were
SUCCESSFUL."

Hero

On July 24, the Apollo 11 team streaked through Earth's atmosphere like a comet. Three **parachutes** burst open above the small pod that contained the three astronauts and their precious load of moon rocks. A few minutes later, the capsule splashed down into the Pacific Ocean.

They were quickly picked up by a navy ship called the USS *Hornet*.

Even before they were helicoptered aboard the *Hornet*, Neil, Buzz and Michael were given special isolation suits to wear. Finally though, they landed on the *Hornet*'s deck and sailors cheered, drowning out the band that was playing. The president was also there, leaning over the rail and waving at the returning astronauts.

Their *journey* was almost over, but before Neil and his crew could return to their families they had to spend two weeks in QUARANTINE.

The three men knew that their journey to the moon had caused a *sensation* back on Earth, but none of them expected what came next.

QUARANTINE:
when someone is kept completely separate from other people – in this instance, in case the astronauts had brought back any alien "space germs" from the moon.

Eventually Neil was allowed to go home to his *family*. He had to fight his way through cheering crowds and TV crews and photographers and reporters.

Neil wasn't given much time to rest. The world wanted to know about his incredible *adventure*.

There were *interviews* and press conferences and personal appearances to do. Neil had never been comfortable in the *spotlight*, but now he was the most famous man in the world: the first man on the moon, a living legend, a *hero*.

During a visit to New York City, millions turned out to watch Neil, Buzz and Michael pass by in an open-top car. The sky was blotted out by streamers and confetti. The cheers were a constant roar. A visit to the city of Chicago was the same. Important people lined up to shake Neil's hand. In Los Angeles, President Nixon threw a huge party. More than 1,000 guests, including Hollywood stars, were invited to meet the astronauts.

For another party – a barbecue in Houston – thousands of people were invited. Next, Neil, Buzz and Michael visited twenty-five countries around the world in forty-five days, meeting presidents and prime ministers, kings and queens (including Queen Elizabeth II). Everywhere they went, Neil and his crewmates were showered with praise.

When the world tour came to an end, Neil wasn't sure what he'd do next. NASA had made it clear he would never go into space again. He was too important now to have his life risked. Fame and money didn't interest him either. When the *attention* finally started to die down, Neil looked for a job that would take him out of the spotlight and back to his first love – *engineering*.

He worked for NASA for a little while, then in 1971 – two years after returning from the moon – he took a job *teaching* aircraft engineering at the University of Cincinnati in Ohio, the state where he had been born.

DID YOU KNOW?

While he was still working for NASA after returning from the moon, Neil helped invent computer navigation technology called "fly-by-wire," which is still used in spacecraft and airplanes today.

"How we use the **knowledge** we gain DETERMINES our progress ON *Earth*, IN *space* OR ON *the moon*. YOUR LIBRARY IS A STOREHOUSE FOR *mind* AND *spirit*. *Use it well.*"

— From a letter to the children of Troy, Michigan, on the opening of a new library.

Looking to the stars

*F*or the rest of his days, Neil tried his best to keep his life *private*. He felt he had been given too much *credit* for an effort that had involved thousands of people.

Have you heard of **Katherine Johnson**? She was one of the most important scientists behind the mission that put Neil and Buzz on the moon.

To him, the fact that he had been first on the moon was almost an accident.

> "*I wasn't chosen* TO BE FIRST. *I was just chosen* TO COMMAND THAT FLIGHT."

Even so, Neil remained *passionate* about space exploration. He traveled the world, giving speeches on the subject.

In 1986 the space shuttle Challenger exploded during a launch, and Neil was part of the team of investigators that worked out what had gone wrong.

He returned to the **public eye** again in 2010, when President Obama **canceled** an expensive plan to return to the moon. Neil spoke out against the decision. He always wanted astronauts to go farther, and thought the next big project should be to land on *Mars* – an actual planet.

Neil never went into space again, but he always kept his *pilot's license* and flew any time he had the chance. He especially loved the *silence* and *freedom* of flying unpowered gliders.

His busy life kept him away from home a lot, and he and Janet divorced in 1994.

Neil soon married **Carol Held Knight**, and the couple lived happily together for the rest of his life.

As he grew older, Neil never stopped working. He went to many scientific events around the world, giving speeches and attending meetings. In the summer of 2012 he made his *final* public appearance. On stage at the Lowell Observatory in Flagstaff, Arizona, he talked 730 guests through Eagle's descent onto the moon while *film* taken at the time was shown on-screen. At the end a recording played Neil's famous line: *"The Eagle has landed."* Every person in the room leaped to their feet to give Neil *thunderous applause.*

In August 2012, just after his eighty-second birthday, Neil was taken to the hospital for a heart operation. He had faced death many times – in the Korean War, as a pilot testing experimental aircraft and in the depths of space – but in the end he died peacefully in a hospital bed. On August 25, 2012, Neil Armstrong's extraordinary life came to an end.

The world *mourned* his passing. Not only was he a hero and a great *explorer* who had proved that humans could walk on the moon, but he was a good man: kind, decent, humble, thoughtful, wise and with a wicked sense of humor.

Newspapers around the world were filled with glowing words from important and famous people, as well as his two crewmates.

"THE
best pilot
I EVER KNEW."

– Buzz Aldrin

"HE WAS THE BEST, AND
I will miss him
TERRIBLY."

– Michael Collins

At his funeral, fighter jets flew in a special formation in tribute. President Obama ordered that all American flags, no matter where in the world they were flying, should be brought to HALF-MAST in his honor.

HALF-MAST: halfway down their pole. People lower flags to half-mast as a sign of respect for a great person who has died.

Soon after his death, Neil's family issued a press release. It said,

"FOR THOSE WHO MAY ASK
what they can do
TO HONOR NEIL . . .

"The next time

YOU WALK OUTSIDE

on a clear night

AND SEE THE MOON

smiling

down at you,

THINK OF
Neil
Armstrong
AND
give him a
WINK."

TIMELINE

August 5, 1930

Neil Alden Armstrong born in Wapakoneta, Ohio.

August 1946

Earns his pilot's license at sixteen.

1947

Neil leaves home at seventeen to study aircraft engineering at Purdue University.

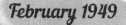

February 1949

Begins training as a pilot in the US Navy.

August 29, 1951

Flies his first mission in the Korean War.

1955

Graduates from college with a degree in engineering and starts work as a test pilot for NACA.

January 1956
Marries Janet Shearon.

1961
Russian astronaut Yuri Gagarin becomes the first man in space.

September 1962
John F. Kennedy makes his famous moon speech. Neil Armstrong joins the US space program.

March 16, 1966
Takes his first flight into space on Gemini 8.

July 16, 1969

Neil Armstrong, Buzz Aldrin and Michael Collins blast off from Kennedy Space Center in Florida.

July 21, 1969

Neil becomes the first man to walk on the moon.

July 24, 1969

Neil, Buzz and Michael splash down in the Pacific Ocean and are met by President Nixon.

1971

Neil leaves NASA to start teaching at the University of Cincinnati.

1986

Neil becomes vice-chairman of the investigation into the explosion of the space shuttle Challenger.

1994

Divorces Janet and marries Carol Held Knight.

May 2010

Joins other NASA astronauts to protest against the cancellation of US space projects.

August 25, 2012
Neil Armstrong dies in
Cincinnati, Ohio.

SOME THINGS TO THINK ABOUT...

It's been more than fifty years since Neil Armstrong walked on the moon, and there's still so much out there to discover. Can you imagine where we might be in another fifty years?

There are many tales that the crew of Apollo 11 saw UFOs while they traveled toward the moon. On the third day Buzz spotted an object flashing in space, as if they were being signaled by an alien ship. Mission Control was confused by their reports – and eventually decided it was part of an old rocket that had been dumped, spinning in space and catching the sunlight. But do you think there was a possibility that Neil and the crew really did see a UFO?

It was a long journey to and from the moon. To pass the time Neil and his crew often played jokes on each other. What would you do to keep yourself entertained?

Neil and Buzz didn't know if they would make it back from the moon alive. What do you think made them take such a risk when they signed up for the mission?

President Nixon had prepared a speech to give in the event that Neil, Buzz and Michael didn't return from the moon. Have you read it?

Index

Quote Sources

There is only one authorized biography of Neil Armstrong, the excellent *First Man: The Life of Neil A. Armstrong*, by James R. Hansen (Simon & Schuster). It was enormously valuable during the writing of this book.

Also of great use were the details of the Apollo 11 mission (including complete transcripts of communications between the crew and Mission Control) on NASA's website – www.nasa.gov

An interview of Neil by Dr. Stephen E. Ambrose and Dr. Douglas Brinkley from NASA's Johnson Space Center Oral History Project was extremely helpful and can be found at www.jsc.nasa.gov

I also referred to several filmed interviews with Neil, which can be found on YouTube, including "Neil Armstrong Interview" (BBC 1970) and "Apollo 11 Crew Interview" (May 25, 1989, NASA).

Quotes were taken from Hansen's book, and from www.brainyquote.com Various snippets of information relating to Neil's life and the Gemini/Apollo missions were also provided by en.wikipedia.org

Have you read about all of these extraordinary people?

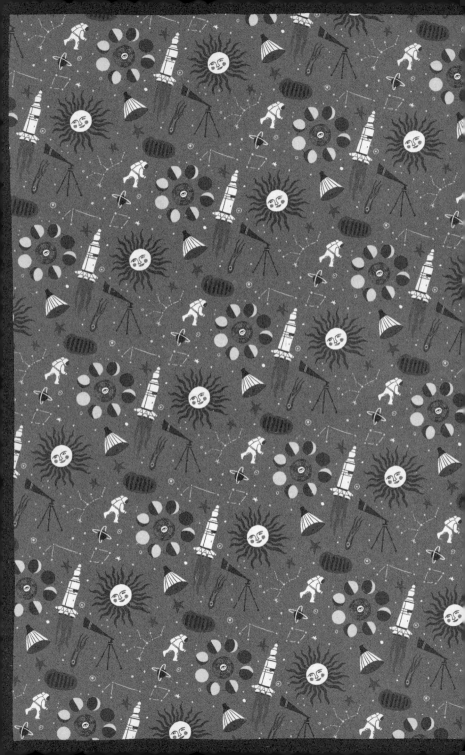

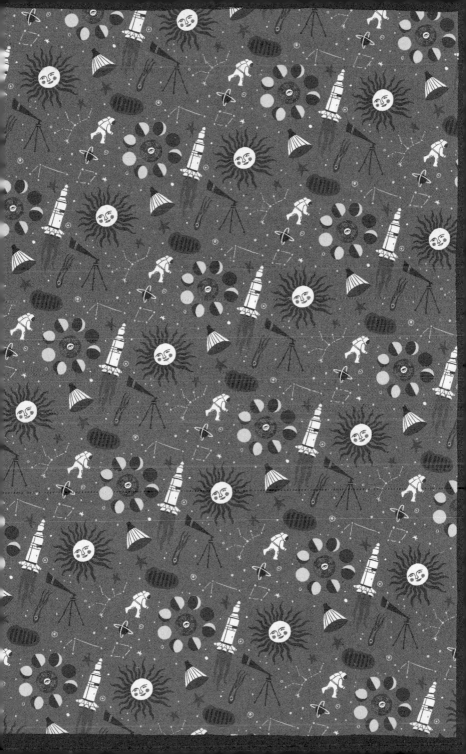